CW00432238

How to Become a Wedding Planner

The Ultimate Guide to a Successful Wedding Planning Career

by Nadia Sullivan

Table of Contents

Introduction

So, you want to become a wedding planner? That's great! You love the glitz and glamor of bridal gowns, fancy invitations, wedding parties, flowers and other decorations. You feel certain you can do it because you have the passion for planning events and paying attention to details. But just keep in mind that success in this business depends on much more than that. Becoming a successful wedding planner entails a LOT of hard work and determination and a bit of business savvy and social skills too.

The good news is that the need for wedding planners nowadays is increasing and the financial and personal rewards are tremendous. Most people will get married at some point in their lives, and many engaged couples require the services of a wedding planner. Hence, it can be a lucrative job if you're the right person.

Busy couples often feel the need to let someone knowledgeable and responsible help them plan for this momentous event that will hopefully happen only once in their lifetime. They're nervous and unable to focus because of excitement, stress, and other obligations going on in their life at the same time, so they need a wedding planner to nit-pick all the details of their wedding and ensure their magical moment comes together flawlessly. That's you! This means you'll become not only a wedding planner, but also a personal assistant, a counselor, and a shock absorber for them. Are you ready for it?

This book will present all of the things you'll need to consider and conquer in order to establish a successful wedding planning business. Let's get started!

© Copyright 2014 by LCPublifish LLC - All rights reserved.

This document is geared towards providing reliable information in regard to the topic and issue covered. The publication is sold with the idea that the publisher is not required to render accounting, officially permitted, or otherwise, qualified services. If advice is necessary, legal or professional, a practiced individual in the profession should be ordered.

- From a Declaration of Principles which was accepted and approved equally by a Committee of the American Bar Association and a Committee of Publishers and Associations.

In no way is it legal to reproduce, duplicate, or transmit any part of this document in either electronic means or in printed format. Recording of this publication is strictly prohibited and any storage of this document is not allowed unless with written permission from the publisher. All rights reserved.

The information provided herein is stated to be truthful and consistent, in that any liability, in terms of inattention or otherwise, by any usage or abuse of any policies, processes, or directions contained within is solely and completely the responsibility of the recipient reader. Under no circumstances will any legal responsibility or blame be held against the publisher for any reparation, damages, or monetary loss due to the information herein, either directly or indirectly.

Respective authors own all copyrights not held by the publisher.

The information herein is offered for informational purposes solely, and is universal as so. The presentation of the information is without contract or any type of guarantee assurance.

The trademarks that are used are without any consent, and the publication of the trademark is without permission or backing by the trademark owner. All trademarks and brands within this book are for clarifying purposes only and are the owned by the owners themselves, not affiliated with this document.

Chapter 1: Traits of a Successful Wedding Planner

Not everyone can be a successful wedding planner. In fact, many have actually tried and failed. They may chalk it up to sheer bad luck or bad timing, but I can assure you that most people's success depends on their determination, persistence and attitude. How is it that some people succeed and some don't? What's the key to their triumph? Experiences of successful people reveal common traits that winners all possess, and these are what you'll have to learn to embody. If you want to become a successful wedding planner, you must acquire the following 10 traits:

Dedication

Successful professionals are dedicated to their craft. They give beyond what's expected of them, without counting the hours. They give one hundred percent to everything they do, leaving no stones unturned. They crave perfection. Dedication means having passion for work. You'll have to emulate this trait too, if you want to succeed in your career as a wedding planner. Be the best in your field by constantly learning and updating your knowledge and giving your best when you work.

Your target should be perfection, even if you have to work long hours (without pay) to attain it. You shouldn't prioritize the monetary benefits, especially if you're still starting out. Once you've gotten your name out there, then monetary rewards will definitely follow. Being dedicated alone doesn't spell success. Without a good plan and proper work ethics, you simply won't succeed.

Persistence

A person who readily gives up because of problems they encounter in their career will never succeed. Think of these problems as challenges you must overcome to make you stronger. If you failed the first time, don't give up. Modify your plan and go for it again, and again, and again, until you succeed. Persistence pays off.

Reliability

Probably the most important trait of a great wedding planner is their reliability, which allows their clients to fully trust them. They must trust that you will pick up the phone when they call, and that you will be there at the exact you agreed to, bringing with you the 12 lace tablecloths, the 3 yellow ribbons, and the 15 samples of cake that you agreed to bring. Without your client's unshakable faith in your dependability, you might as well just go home and start searching the classified ads for a different job.

Attentiveness

Your clients should be content and happy with your services. Be attentive to what they want. Don't insist on your ideas, unless necessary. You can make suggestions to achieve better results to their objectives, but take note that each person has unique needs and preferences; therefore, you should always listen first to what they want. Be receptive to the clients' verbal and non-verbal messages. This will help a lot in creating the best wedding, based on your clients' wishes.

Resourcefulness

Resourcefulness is one trait that you should cultivate. Couples will, definitely, appreciate it if you come up with ways to cut the cost of the event – unless they're filthy rich, of course. When sudden problems crop up during the planning, you should be able to remedy it without causing too much fuss or exacerbating costs. Remedy small problems with practical solutions.

Ingenuity

Ingenuity is vital when you're a wedding planner. Strive to be original, as much as possible. Don't imitate the plans of another, just because it was successful. Tap into your creativity, and together with the couple's suggestions, come up with a wedding scenario that's unique and beautiful. Every couple wants their wedding to be the unique wedding that everyone will be talking about, so work on this premise and you'll never go wrong.

Amiability

You should be amiable, so clients won't feel threatened. You'll be more likable, and your clients will feel relaxed and glad they choose you as their wedding planner. Smile and show them you're truly honored to give them the best of your services.

Honesty

As the cliché says, "Honesty is the best policy." When you're honest with your clients, they'll learn to trust you. If the wedding dress that the bride picked doesn't fit well, then you'll have to tell her honestly, but diplomatically. It's not what you say but how you say it that counts.

Sincerity

Sincerity makes actions valid. Show your clients you sincerely want to help them make their wedding ceremony, the best - and mean it. They'll surely notice this, and will feel relieved and glad that they have a wedding planner to whom they can open up, and they can trust.

Being Observant

Being a wedding planner, you must be observant to details. Wedding ceremonies need lots of attention; a misplaced button or pin can lead to catastrophe, or an upset Bride. A misspelled name can be embarrassing. You should be observant, so you can notice any small error before it becomes one big mistake.

If you think you already possess these traits, or that you could cultivate them, then, by all means, pursue your dreams of becoming a wedding planner. There's a great chance you'll succeed! Later on in your career, when clients observe how dedicated, honest and sincere you are; they'll recommend you to their families and friends, and your network will expand exponentially.

Chapter 2: Building a Career as a Wedding Planner

Every house construction begins by building a solid foundation. Likewise, in your career, you'll have to build a solid foundation. It should be strong and able to withstand any type of pressure later on.

You can do this by acquiring expertise in your career. It's understandable that you will start as a novice without any experience, but strive to learn all about being a wedding planner before anything else. To help you with this endeavor, here are some steps you can follow.

Enroll in a legitimate wedding planning course

You could learn by experience, but that would take a long time. You should consider enrolling in a legitimate and reliable wedding planning course. There are several courses online that can provide you this service. You don't even need to be physically present. Most of these courses, also, provide actual exposure and a certificate after you finish the course. Choose the online provider of the course judiciously. Ascertain that they're legitimate and reliable. Of course, you can enroll in a school near your area, if there is one. Nothing beats hands-on learning.

Although there are no state boards or licensure exams for wedding planners, a valid certificate proving you've undergone training can help you significantly in getting your name out there, and making potential clients feel more comfortable with your level of expertise. Your training will also give you the confidence to be sure that you know what you're doing.

Here are some online schools, you can select from:

- New York Institute of Arts and Design – offers a variety of courses, which include Wedding Event Planning. (www.nyiad.edu/courses/wedding-event-planning)

- Weddings Beautiful Worldwide – provides courses for wedding planners and specialists. (http://www.weddingsbeautiful.com/cwp2.asp)

- Sheffield School – provides an array of short courses, including wedding planning.

16

(www.sheffield.edu/htmlsrc/wedding-event-planning-course.html)

- ed2go Career Planning Center – offers various courses, which include wedding planning. (www.ed2go.com/career/training-programs/wedding-planner-course)

Learn from previous experts

During your learning period, you can volunteer as an assistant to an expert in wedding planning. Glean as much skill and information as possible from this expert. If this is not possible, you can search online and read about the experiences of wedding planners around the world. Write down any important information, especially juicy tips, so you won't forget it. Subscribe to an online wedding planners' magazine or journal to receive free copies. Buy magazines and acquaint yourself with what other wedding planners are busy with.

After you've gained more experience, and feel that you could tutor other people interested in wedding planning, then you could eventually become a wedding consultant – helping mentor others who want to become wedding planners. This can take a long time, but it's one option you may consider.

Join wedding planners' organizations

You can enlist your name in online yellow pages, or join wedding planners' organizations, where you can interact, exchange ideas and learn from your colleagues. Be open to new ideas and be ready to assimilate all useful information that you encounter.

Practice your craft

Be brave and ready to grab any opportunity to practice your craft. Why not start with the weddings of your family and friends? Volunteer as a wedding planner to get your feet wet. Then, once you've gained some experience, you can accept other jobs for pay. Your first job may be terrifying, if you allow it to be. Be confident that you can do it because you have prepared yourself well, and you know you will be able to find a creative solution to any problem at a moment's notice. You may make a few mistakes on your first try, but simply learn from these mistakes and keep going. For each wedding that you have successfully planned, your confidence and self-worth will increase. So, will your value as a wedding planner, and consequentially, your pay scale.

Chapter 3: How to Establish Your Own Wedding Planning Business

Now that you're ready to expand your career a little further, you can establish a business of your own as a wedding planner. If you've decided to proceed with this superb plan, you'll have to attend to it - fulltime. Before you continue, however, you'll first have to make a plan.

What are the first things that you should do? You can't just put up a business without sufficient funding or enough manpower. Luckily for a wedding planning business, you don't need a big capital account or numerous people to run it. You don't need an elaborate office; you can use a small corner of your apartment for your work. You also won't need an assistant at the onset. Perhaps, as your service becomes more and more popular, and you have multiple bookings per week, then you can hire an assistant or a secretary.

Here are 6 useful steps that will help you establish your business:

Step #1 - Ensure that your business is legal

The first thing that you must do is to ensure that your business is legal and is registered with the appropriate licensing organization in your state. You can ask the help of a competent lawyer in this aspect. He can explain to you whatever documents and requirements you need for your wedding planning business. Your certificate showing you have undergone a course in wedding planning may help facilitate this process.

You can request that your lawyer draw up contracts for you and your client so that your rights and your clients' rights are protected. Go over the contracts and licenses of your business carefully with your lawyer. Your business tax is one item you really must look into. There may be differences in the issuance of business permits in some locations, so be sure to know all about these too.

Step #2 - Set your business goals

You can't plan properly if you don't have goals. Goals will give direction to how your business ought to proceed. Set short and long-term goals, so you can assess your progress easily. These will keep your business on the right track.

Examples of goals are:

- 90% positive reviews for first 3 months of operation (short term goal)

- Land your first wedding event in the two weeks of operation (short term goal)

- 70% increase of clients, after a year of operation (long term goal)

- Establishment of a wedding clothing and accessory store after 5 years (long term goal)

In setting goals, be specific. Use a definite time frame. You can utilize the SMART method in preparing your goals:

S – Specific (goals should be specific)

M – Measurable (you can easily assess the progress)

A – Attainable (you can achieve them, they're not impossible)

R – Relevant (the goals are related to what your business wants to achieve)

T – Time-bound (there are definitive time/dates for the completion of the goals)

In doing so, you can immediately assess if your goals have been achieved or not.

Step #3 – Create a brand for your business

In the process of registering your business, you can create a brand for your business. What do you want to achieve as a business entity? Based on this, you can derive your business name, slogan and logo. Your stationery and all of your products and communications must use this brand to easily identify your business from others.

Your business name must be short but appealing. A logo that's simple but eye-catching will help you market your services too. Both should be based on your business brand. A good example is the brand of the famous company, Apple Incorporation. The logo of the company is an apple that has a small portion of it, apparently, bitten, and its recent slogan is "*Think different*"; short, snappy and rich with meaning.

Business related products can come out of your brand, namely: wedding gifts, wedding gowns, and other wedding items.

Step #4 – Advertise your business

Advertising is vital to the success of a business. After you've set everything up, advertise, advertise, and advertise. Even if you're the best wedding planner on the face of the earth, if no one knows about you, then it's useless. Word-of-mouth is the best promotion technique, but it's not as fast as advertising directly online and offline. Before advertising, create various example wedding planning packages to respond to each client's needs and financial capabilities. This will facilitate transactions between you and your client. You can read the different methods of advertising in Chapter 4.

Step #5 – Keep in touch with your clients

It's imperative that you keep in touch with your previous and present clients. Keep your lines open 24/7. This demonstrates your genuine concern about them as individuals. Your clients have friends and relatives to whom they will recommend you based on their experiences with you. If they learn that you're the best in what you do, they'll recommend you to everyone they know. Your previous clients are your most trusted team of advertisers through word-of-mouth marketing.

Step #6 – Assess achievements

Based on your goals, remember to do assessment checks, regularly. If your short-term goals are on a weekly basis, then assess weekly. A monthly basis, though, is more convenient for new entrepreneurs. It's up to you; just make sure that your goals are achieved in the specified time you have designated.

After assessment, you can modify your goals to accommodate or improve your outcomes. Determine your problem areas and improve them by realigning your goals. You won't succeed unless you have SMART goals.

Chapter 4: How to Advertise Your Business

If you want to leave no stone unturned for the success of your business, this is one aspect you must concentrate on – advertising. You can do it online and offline. It doesn't matter as long as you get the word out there. Choose the least expensive but most effective advertising technique. There are a number of them you can select from. Take your time and choose wisely. The most ideal is to use all of these methods and go on a blitzkrieg campaign, at least until you have a booked schedule for the foreseeable future. This would facilitate the advertisement of your wedding planning services to all people, simultaneously.

Here are effective techniques you can use to advertise your services:

Create a website

It's wise to create a website and/or a blog for your wedding planning business. The cost is minimal; the webhosting fees and website themes will cost you less than a hundred dollars a month for shared servers. Webhosting fees cost around $3 to $10 a month for shared servers and around $140 to $300 a month for dedicated servers, depending on your preferences.

For your small-time wedding planning business, the shared servers will be fine. This is because your clients list is still minimal. In fact, even the free hosting sites are sufficient, if you're strapped financially. Wordpress.com and Blogger.com offer free webhosting services. The shared servers, nonetheless, is the best for your small-time business. If you're not sure where to start, SquareSpace has a platform that is very user friendly and you will be able to easily create an elegant website in just a day or two on your own, and as of the time of writing this book, costs are in the neighborhood of $100 per year.

These days, online advertising is the easiest, most convenient and cheapest way to advertise. Through your website, you can present your portfolio consisting of your certificates, training programs, professional memberships, previous wedding planning events, photos of these events, reliable references, and client reviews. Remember to add your contact details and email address so that potential clients can easily get in touch with you.

You can also create a blog page and post articles about wedding events, and a Q & A (Questions and Answers) portion to enhance the readability and helpfulness of your website. Moreover, written positive testimonials from your clients will increase your credibility.

Advertise on Facebook, Twitter, Pinterest and LinkedIn

Advertising on Facebook, Twitter, Pinterest and LinkedIn is proven to be very effective. You can create a page using your brand name, logo and slogan. You can post pictures of your past accomplishments, or photos of mock weddings. You can also include a list of your discount packages or freebies, if any.

Tweeting about your services will help you advertise too; many businesses flourish using these social media sites. There are online applications that allow you to automatically tweet your services such as TwitterFeed, TweetAdder, and Hootsuite. You can program the application with what to tweet and at what time the tweet will appear during the day. You don't have to spent considerable time doing this, and it's free. There are also paid advertising tweets, but why spend when you can avail of it for free?

A Facebook (FB) page is a great advertising method. It's easy and it's free, as well. Advertisers find Facebook more interactive than Twitter and LinkedIn as their clients can interact with them through the FB comment page. You'll have to prioritize opening a page on FB, so you can allow your clients to post comments. You'll be able to reply quickly to their posts too. The "Like" button will help promote your page; the more "Likes", the more chances of being viewed by your FB followers.

LinkedIn works the same way as Twitter. Your LinkedIn page will reveal some information about what you do. You can post a link to your business website, and readers can click the link to visit it. LinkedIn is more of a website for professionals, so there are career groups there which you could join in and exchange ideas with.

On the other hand, Pinterest provides a venue for you to post pictures of your business. Display vivid and colorful images to visually attract more Pinterest users. Users can also share your photos, if they find them worth sharing. Put your best shots forward, and let the world advertise them for you. These are all free services that you must take advantage of.

Use business cards or flyers

Offline, you can distribute business cards, brochures, or flyers to let your local community know about your services. Prepare business cards reflecting your brand, remember to add your contact information such as, cell phone number, email address, and website address. Your physical address may also be included. On the card you can add a short but meaningful slogan to attract clients. It's preferable to use your business slogan, so that it can become a common household phrase.

Enlist your business in the Yellow Pages

As mentioned in Chapter 2, your name, as a wedding planner, must be included in the yellow pages of the phone directory. You can list your company's name too, under the wedding planning services category. The telephone directory is still one of the first contact information resources that people resort to when searching for services. Double check if your name is included in the online version of the yellow pages.

Enlist your business in other Wedding Planner Associations

There are certain states that have organized an association for wedding planners. Check these out and join all of them. This is one way to effectively advertise your services. When your name is not included in any of these organizations, clients may not know of you or your services. Don't allow this to happen, become a member and enjoy the privileges that come with it. Some of these associations are:

- American Association of Certified Wedding Planners (AACWP) (www.aacwp.org)

- Association of Certified Professional Wedding Consultants (ACPWC) (www.acpwc.com)

- Association for Wedding Professionals International (AWPI) (www.*afwpi.com*)

Advertise in newspapers and magazines

Place an ad in your local papers and magazines. The cost will depend on how big your page will be. Advertising in magazines are costly but can capture another set of clients – your reading clients. You can post photo shoots of a mock wedding to show prospective clients your expertise. In addition, you can advertise in a national magazine for worldwide exposure, but be ready to travel anywhere when a client requires your services.

Use radio stations

This can be free of charge, or it can be expensive depending on your agreement with the radio station owners. This is a good method to reach people who have no time to read. Some advertisers tend to think radio is a waste of time; it's not. Somebody who's listening on the radio while driving can easily end up being your client, especially if they're impressed or captivated by what you have to say, or how you say it. Imagine all the countless commuters and radio listeners as your clients. Prepare brief but appealing phrases for your radio listeners. When they tune in and listen to your advertisement, you can capture their attention. Be sure to let them know how to get in touch with you – and in a way, that's something they can memorize instead of having to write down (remember, they're driving). If you know your website comes up when you google your name, then tell them to google your name. Or if your website address is simple, then repeat it a few times for them. Or maybe the radio station will agree to put up a temporary link to your website on their own website for a few days, so you can tell the listener to go to the radio station's website for a direct link to yours.

Attend events

Grab the chance to mingle with potential clients. Share your business experiences during events such as parties, weddings, and holiday celebrations. You can also hand out your business cards during the affair. Be discreet about it, though, it's not good manners to disrupt an event to advertise your own business.

Participate in trade shows

Some trade shows offer free booth spaces, some don't. Learn about the details and prepare for it days before the actual event. Rent a booth or a stall to let people know about your services. Bring along your wedding photos, business cards and flyers. Display your best materials to show clients that your services are reliable and trustworthy. You can prepare a short video presentation for interested people.

Use TV advertising

Television is a powerful medium for advertising, but it's also the most expensive. Perhaps, when you become highly successful, you can utilize TV, complete with images and actors. Big companies produce videos featuring popular celebrities, who advertise their services. You can do this too; don't worry – but take things one step at a time. It's free to dream, so dream big. You can do anything you sincerely desire so work on your business with this positive thought in mind.

Volunteer to organize a charity event for free

This method will target your local community. You can organize an event in your community for free. You can request the help of your health professionals to conduct free medical missions, where doctors provide free consultations for patients. Your dance instructor friends can also conduct free dance lessons for the benefit of the youth in your community. You may also offer discounted prices for your first, three wedding planning services, or you can give it for free, just to get your name out there. Use your wise judgment on what's best for the people in your area.

Use business posters

Prepare a poster that gives a bird's eye view of your business. It should be visually and graphically attractive to make people read it. Red, yellow, green and blue colors are considered eye-catching, but you must consider the logo of your business. The logo and slogan should always appear in your advertising materials. Don't forget to include your contact information so that clients can contact you. Post them in all areas where you're allowed to do so.

There are countless methods to advertise your services. You have to use your resourcefulness and creativity to think of various other forms that can be applicable in your wedding planning business.

Chapter 5: Other Important Tips & Reminders

Congratulations! You're now ready to start your own business as a successful wedding planner. Review the steps mentioned in the previous chapters carefully and implement them.

As a final measure, below are important reminders and key pointers you must keep in mind if you want to succeed in your chosen career as a wedding planner:

- **Acquire and maintain a positive outlook**

  A positive outlook is needed in any undertaking. When you're an optimist, your chances of succeeding will increase considerably. You perceive problems as exciting challenges and opportunities, making it easier for you to overcome them. You're not scared to implement innovations meant to improve your services.

  People and clients will want to be around you because you radiate positive energy and aura.

You're a winner and the world loves winners. Being optimistic takes constant practice if you've been a pessimist for a long time. Getting rid of that negative attitude can be taxing, but you can do it. You can change, as long as you put your heart and mind into it. Strive to be positive in everything that you do, and the positive vibes will reflect back to you through your success.

- **Build relationships because they are essential to your success**

Yes, your relationships with other people can dictate your success or failure. Perceive people as either potential clients, or potential marketers on your behalf. Once you've got to know them, you should deal with them sincerely. Spend time befriending your fellow wedding planners. That way you can count on them for support. They can back you up as references in the future. Your primary motivation in cultivating these relationships shouldn't be financial gain, though; you must build your relationships because you sincerely want to.

- **Charge your clients reasonably and appropriately**

  Make a survey of how much wedding planners charge their clients. Based on this, prepare a reasonable fee for your services. It's advisable to strike a balance between what you can offer comfortably and the paying capability of your client. You can provide discounted prices for your first clients, if it is possible to do so. Use your good judgment for better results.

- **Landing your first client is always the hardest, but you'll get by**

  Getting your first client will prove to be the most difficult because you're still trying to establish your career. Nevertheless, once you've landed your first clients, the next ones will be easier. If you gave all your best to your first clients, then your business will be selling like hot cakes in the long run.

- **As a small business owner, be prepared to multi-task**

Expect to be multi-tasking because you're still starting. Often, you'll act as an assistant to the couple, a secretary, a treasurer, and at times, a gofer. Go the extra mile and be generous with your help. Don't be too concerned about your working hours. Your clients will notice you putting in the extra effort and time and they'll appreciate it. They'll recommend you to another couple in a heartbeat.

- **Stick to your goals**

Prepare your goals carefully so that you can bravely stick with them when the going gets tough. Your goals will serve as your map on the road to success. You need a detailed and specific "map" to succeed.

- **Think of expanding your business**

You can expand your wedding planning business to other related businesses, as mentioned in Chapter 3. With resources, you can successfully branch out to a wedding clothing business or a wedding gift's store within your wedding planning services. Also, the inclusion of bridal tours to your services is a huge but possible expansion. However, you'll have to provide the best wedding planning services first, before you can start the other businesses. Spreading yourself too thin at the start can backfire and cause your downfall. Be a smart entrepreneur, and take things one step at a time.

- **Continue enriching your knowledge**

After you have obtained your certification, don't stop there. Continue learning and updating yourself with new information. There are innovations every day. You can also contribute by introducing your new ideas to improve the wedding planning services. Every day is a learning experience.

- **Enjoy what you're doing**

Lastly, enjoy and be happy with your career. Have fun! When you don't enjoy working, it will be a daily burden for you; no one should live like that. But if you love what you're doing, it's like you're having fun while making money. Isn't that wonderful? So, go out there, and get paid for doing what you love the most.

Conclusion

Becoming a wedding planner is one of the most fulfilling and exciting careers you can embark on. It requires a raft of traits including dedication and honesty for you to succeed. Likewise, building relationships and going out of your way to satisfy your client will increase your chances of succeeding in the business. They all play key roles in your career.

Be the best wedding planner by constantly updating your knowledge and skills with innovations and new technology. Maximize the free applications online for your advertisements to cut cost but simultaneously providing optimum information of your services.

Your ultimate goal is client satisfaction, hence; strive to give your best service, at all times. Your passion for your work will give you enormous rewards eventually. It may take years before you can truly enjoy the fruits of your labor, but it's certain that you'll acquire financial and personal rewards in the future.

Last, I'd like to thank you for reading this book! If you enjoyed it or found it helpful, I'd greatly appreciate it if you'd take a moment to leave a review on Amazon. Thank you!

Printed in Poland
by Amazon Fulfillment
Poland Sp. z o.o., Wrocław

55773572R00031